'NORFOLK COAST AND COU

Including Sheringham, Felbrigg, Crome Wildlife Park, Castle Acre, Castle Rising Brancaster, The Burnhams, Holkham Blakeney, Weybourne, Holt

This guide contains exact, but simple c wishes to combine visits to such well known places as Sandringham, Wells, Sheringham and Cromer with an exploration of the small towns and villages that lie hidden beyond the network of main roads.

The 'Main Circle' Route (Maps 1 – 12) shown on the Key Map opposite covers 120 miles, most of which are through quiet, unspoilt countryside. This route can be approached with ease from any of the Norfolk holiday areas, including the Broadland area. You will find that the strip maps show the A roads approaching from the towns, thus giving you an easy link with 'civilization'.

The 'Main Circle' Route is much too long for a leisurely day's journey, and we have included 'link routes' to break this up into smaller circles. You will also find it easy to construct your own routes by making use of the various A roads shown on the Key Map opposite, to link across between two sections of our route.

HOW TO USE YOUR BOOK ON THE ROUTE

Each double page makes up a complete picture of the country ahead of you. On the left you will find a one inch to the mile strip map, with the route marked by a series of dashes. Direction is always from top to bottom, so that the map may be looked at in conjunction with the 'directions...column', with which it is cross referenced by a letter itemising each junction point. This enables the driver to have exact guidance every time an opportunity for changing direction occurs, even if it is only 'Keep straight, not left!'

With mileage intervals shown, the driver should even have warning when to expect those 'moments of decision', and if a sign post exists we have used this to help you, with the 'Sign-Posted...' column. However re-signing is always in progress, and this may lead to slight differences in sign marking in some cases... So beware of freshly erected signs.

We have also included a description of the towns and villages through which you will pass, together with some photographs to illustrate the route.

To gain full enjoyment from your journeys be prepared to leave your car as often as possible. On the coast there are small harbours, sandy shores, wide dunes, creeks, and bird haunted marshes to be explored, while inland there are castles, priories, a wealth of splendid parish churches, as well as several great country houses. This area is now well served with long distance footpaths — The Peddars Way, which runs in a north-westerly direction up to the coast at Holme-next-the-Sea, and the Norfolk Coast Path which runs eastwards from Holme to Cromer along this shoreline rich with wildlife. But whatever your objective, drive slowly, and pause often to observe the special quality of those wide Norfolk horizons, and to sample the quiet pleasures that this fine county has to offer.

COMPILED BY PETER AND HELEN TITCHMARSH
PHOTOGRAPHY BY ALAN AND PETER TITCHMARSH

Map 1

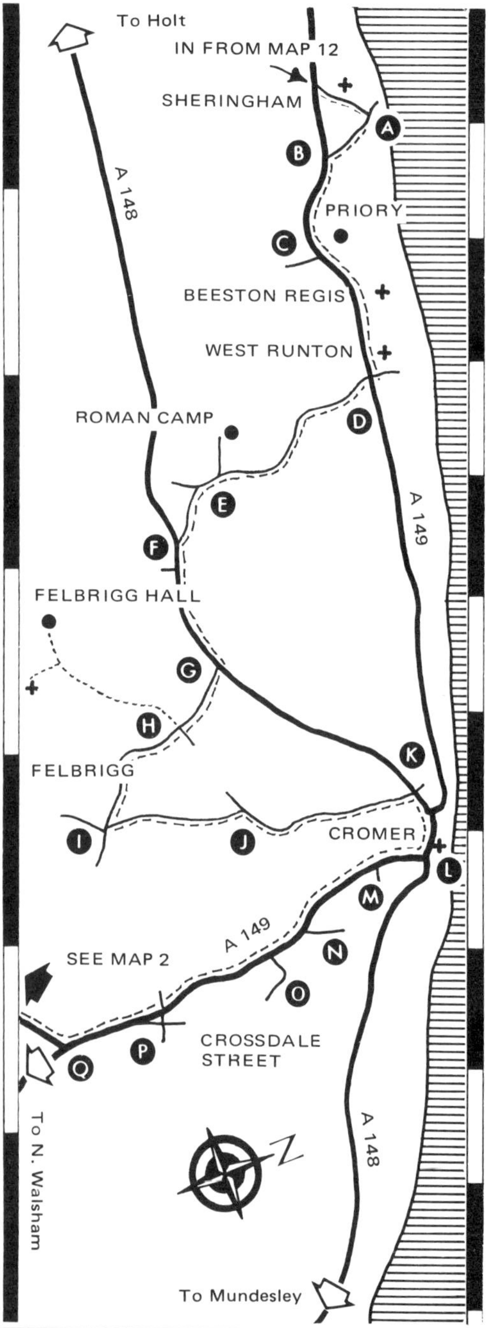

Ref.	kms / Miles	Directions	Sign-posted
A		Depart from Sheringham sea front by the Crown Inn	No sign
		Turn left, and left again, by the Lobster Inn	No sign
	.2	Bear right	Cromer
B	.3	Turn left on to A149	No sign
	.2	Ruins of priory over to left	
	.1	Beeston Regis entry signed	
C	.2	Straight, not right, keeping on A149	Cromer
	.3	Entry to Beeston Regis church on left	
	.1	West Runton entry signed	
	.2	West Runton church on left	
D	.1	Turn right at X rds. in West Runton	Aylmerton
		(But turn left if you wish to visit beach)	
	.4	Up hill into woodlands	
	.5	Track on right to 'Roman Camp'	
E	.1	Fork left	Cromer
F	.3	Turn left, on to A148	Cromer
	.1	Straight, not right	No sign
G	.7	Turn right on to B1436	Norwich
H	.3	Straight, not left at T junction	No sign
		(Entrance to Felbrigg Hall and church on right)	
I	.7	Turn left at X rds.	Cromer
J	.7	Bear right at Y junction Cromer entry signed	Cromer
K	.8	Turn left into 'one-way system' by Allen's Garage	No sign
	.1	Straight, not right at T junction	Hunstanton
		Turn right at sea front	No sign
		Keep straight over small X rds, by Hotel de Paris	No sign
		Straight, not left by church	No sign
	.3	Turn left at T junction by church	No sign
L	.1	Straight, not left, by Albion Hotel	No sign
	.1	Straight, not left, at traffic lights, on to A149 (Follow out of Cromer on A149 for 1 mile)	Norwich
M	.3	Straight, not left	Norwich
N	.5	Straight, not left at Y junction	Norwich
O	.2	Straight, not left	Norwich
P	.6	Over offset X rds. in Crossdale Street hamlet	Norwich
Q	.5	Turn right, on to A140 (Keep on A140 for 3 miles)	Norwich
		Total mileage on this map: 8.9	

CROWN COPYRIGHT RESERVED

On Route

Sheringham
Pleasant seaside resort which grew up in the 1890's and 1900's, with a flavour of the little fishing village upon which it was based, still lingering. Crabbing and fishing are in fact still carried on here and there is a life-boat station at the western end of the beach. Fine cliffs look out over wide stretches of beach. The old railway station houses a museum of steam 'railwayana', and a collection of historic locomotives and rolling stock. Steam trains run from here to Weybourne in the summer season, operated by the North Norfolk Railway Company.

1. Sheringham

Beeston Regis Priory
The ruins of this eleventh century Augustinian priory church are visible from our route, and are attractively sited beside a pond.

Beeston Regis Church
Stands by itself overlooking the sea, a short walk to the left of our route. It has an interesting 15th century screen with painted figures.

West Runton
Residential village situated in wooded countryside, with cliffs overlooking a shingly beach, with sand at low tide. The church has been heavily restored, but we liked the beautiful font cover. Do not miss a visit to the Norfolk Shire Horse Centre, at the West Runton Stables.

2. The 'Roman Camp'

The 'Roman Camp' (National Trust)
This is in fact the site of a beacon, and latterly a telegraph station, and was definitely not a Roman camp. However it is the focal point of over seventy acres of National Trust owned heathland, with glorious stretches of birch trees, gorse and bracken.

Felbrigg Hall (National Trust)
Lovely 17th century country house in mellow brick, with stone dressing, standing in a beautifully wooded park. The interior is rich with fine plasterwork, furniture and paintings. The Hall looks across Humphrey Repton's park to the exquisite little church, which has a perfectly unspoilt Georgian flavour, with painted box pews, and handsome monuments. There is also an outstanding series of brasses dating from 1351. Do not overlook the modest memorial tablet to Mr. K. W. Ketton Cremer whose generosity provided Felbrigg for our delight.

3. Felbrigg Hall

Cromer
Although the majority of Cromer grew up at the same time as Sheringham, the 1890's and early 1900's, there was some 'sea-side' development of the little medieval fishing village much earlier in the 19th century. This older part of Cromer is all within a short distance of its splendidly towered church, and has a pleasantly genuine flavour. On the beach below the cliffs there are boats belonging to the crabmen and fishermen, and from the pier is launched the life-boat, Henry Bloggs... named after Cromer's legendary coxswain.

4. Cromer

Map 2

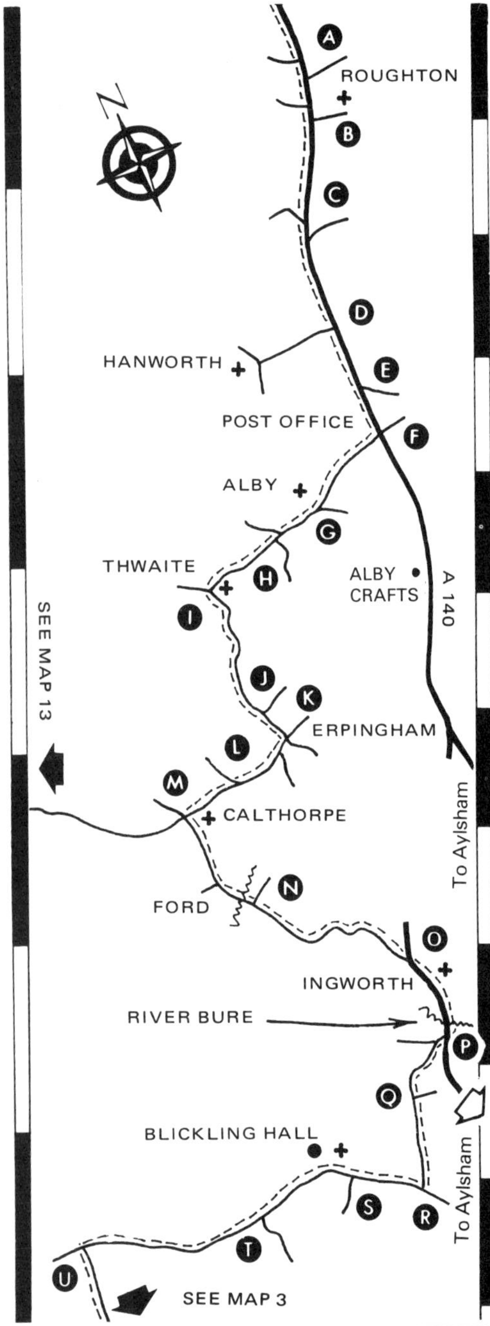

Miles	Ref.	kms / Miles	Directions	Sign-posted
		.2	Roughton entry signed	
	A	.9	Over offset X rds. in Roughton	Norwich
	B	.3	Over small X rds. (But turn left if you wish to visit Roughton church)	Norwich
	C	.6	Over offset X rds.	Norwich
	D	.4	Straight, not right (But turn right if you wish to visit Hanworth church)	Norwich
	E	.4	Straight, not left	Norwich
	F	.2	Turn right at T junction, off A140, by Post Office (But go straight ahead for about 1 mile if you wish to visit Alby Crafts)	Matlaske
		.3	Straight, not right, at T junction	No sign
	G	.5	Straight, not left by Alby church	No sign
	H	.2	Over X rds.	Aldborough
		.4	Thwaite church on left	
	I	.1	Turn left at T junction	No sign
	J	.7	Bear right at T junction	No sign
	K	.2	Turn right at T junction in Erpingham	No sign
		.1	Bear right by the Eagle Inn	Aldborough
	L	.3	Straight, not right	Wolterton
		.3	Calthorpe church on left	
	M	.1	Turn left at X rds. (BUT GO STRAIGHT OVER TO COMMENCE MAP 13)	Ingworth
		.3	Straight, not right, at T junction	No sign
	N	.2	Bear right at T junction beyond ford	No sign
	O	1.0	Bear right, on to wider road, in Ingworth	Aylsham
		.1	Straight, not left, by church Over River Bure	Aylsham
	P	.3	Turn right, off wider road	Blickling
		.1	Fork left	Blickling
	Q	.3	Straight, not left	No sign
	R	.4	Turn right, on to B1354	Blickling
	S	.4	Straight, not left by Blickling church	No sign
		.1	Blickling Hall on right	
		.1	Buckinghamshire Arms on right	
	T	.4	Straight, not left, keeping on B1354 Through pleasant woodlands	No sign
		.9	Open woodlands, with picnic possibilities	
	U	.2	Turn left at T junction	Oulton Street
			Total mileage on this map: 10.7	

CROWN COPYRIGHT RESERVED

4

On Route

Roughton Church
Its tower is Anglo-Saxon, but there is little else of real interest, apart from the odd sculptures on the walls of the nave. (Usually locked.)

Hanworth
The church is not exceptional, but it is prettily sited on a bend in the road, with views beneath the trees to the handsome early 18th century Hanworth Hall... an example of English landscape at its very best. Do not miss the quaint inscription on the memorial in the church to William Doughty, who, *'after eleven years travell into ye Barbados and other Trancemarine Countries safely arrived at his native towne, and when he had with great joy seene all his Friends and Neighbours, took his leave and returned to ye universall place ye Earth, where all must rest till ye sound of ye Trump'*... all rather sad.

Alby Crafts
Nine craft workshops, a gallery displaying a wide range of British-made crafts products, and a tea room. Do not miss a visit here.

Alby Church
Stands in an overgrown churchyard, with its 15th century tower hemmed in by trees. Its interior is not of great interest.

Thwaite Church
Has a Norman round tower and a pleasant prospect from its south porch. The white painted interior contains a reasonable Jacobean pulpit, and some simple poppy head bench ends. However most visitors come here to look at the fine 15th century brass of John Puttock and his wife, buried in the south aisle that they probably built.

Calthorpe
Another unexceptional village, but the church here has a pleasing interior, with 15th century bench ends and (more unusually) benches, a good Jacobean pulpit, and a magnificent font with four lions at its base. The font is also enhanced by a tall, beautifully carved and painted font cover. Between here and Ingworth is an attractive sunken lane overhung with trees, and beyond it, a small ford... all quiet, unspoilt countryside.

Ingworth
We saw swans and gulls on the meadows beyond the watermill at this prettily sited village on the banks of the Bure. The little thatched church has box pews in light oak, a handsomely carved coat of arms of William III, and a pleasantly mellowed floor of old bricks.

Blickling Church
Large church situated close to Blickling Hall. It was extensively restored by the Victorians and is very grand inside. See especially the fine series of brasses (under mats... rubbing by written appointment only), especially Nicholas Dagworth (1401), the font, ornamented with no fewer than twelve lions, and the opulent white marble tomb to the Eighth Marquess of Lothian.

Blickling Hall (See Page 7)

1. Ford beyond Calthorpe

2. Ingworth Church

3. River Bure at Ingworth

4. Blickling Hall

4. Gardens at Blickling

Map 3

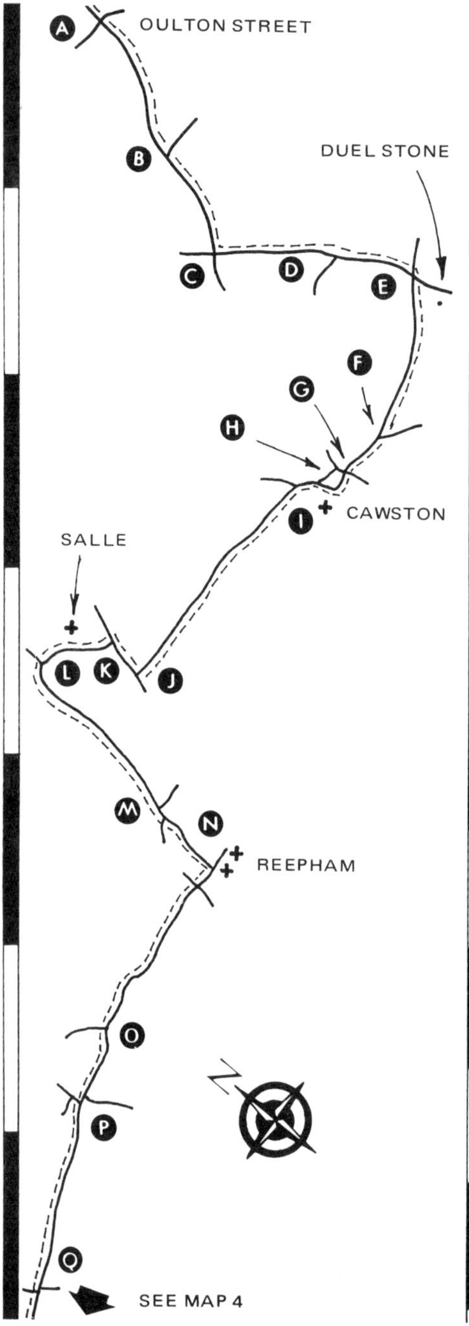

kms Ref. Miles | Directions | Sign-posted

A	.7	Over X rds. into Oulton Street	Cawston
	.6	Disused airfield on right	
B	.3	Straight, not left	Cawston
C	.6	Turn left at X rds., on to B1149	Norwich
D	.7	Straight, not right	No sign
E	.4	Turn right at X rds., on to B1145 (But go straight over if you wish to visit the Duel Stone)	Reepham
F	.4	Straight, not left	Reepham
G	.6	Bear right beyond entry to Cawston	Reepham
	.2	Fork left, off B1145	Brandiston
H	.1	Over X rds.	New Street
	.1	Turn right by church and... Turn left beyond church rejoining B1145	No sign No sign
I	.2	Bear left beyond railway bridge	Reepham
J	1.4	Turn right, off B1145	Heydon
K	.2	Turn left at T junction	Wood Dalling
	.2	Salle church on right	
L	.3	Bear left at T junction	Reepham
	1.0	Entering Reepham	
M	.1	Straight, not left, rejoining B1145	Bawdeswell
	.1	Fork left, keeping Crown Inn on left	'Olland's Rd.'
N	.3	Turn right at T junction by churches, and... Through Square	No sign
	.1	Over small X rds., rejoining B1145	Bawdeswell
O	1.0	Bear left, keeping on B1145	Bawdeswell
P	.5	Over X rds., keeping on B1145	Bawdeswell
Q	1.1	Over X rds., keeping on B1145	Bawdeswell
		Total mileage on this map: 11.2	

CROWN COPYRIGHT RESERVED

On Route

Blickling Hall (National Trust) (See Page 4)
Splendid Jacobean mansion in mellow brick, built for Sir Henry Hobart, who was Chief Justice of Common Pleas in the reign of James I. The interior was partly altered in the late 18th century, although the Great Gallery still retains its fine Jacobean plaster ceiling, and many other 17th century features remain. This is one of Norfolk's finest country houses and contains an excellent collection of furniture, pictures and tapestry. See also the formal gardens with the classical temple beyond, and the beautifully wooded park with its crescent shaped lake.

1. The Duel Stone, near Cawston

The Duel Stone (National Trust)
A small stone urn situated in a coppice to the right of the road, a quarter of a mile beyond Point F. This commemorates a duel fought between Henry Hobart of Blickling Hall and Oliver La Neve of Great Witchingham Hall... the result of an election quarrel.

Cawston
Pleasant little town with many satisfying small houses of mellow brick... all overshadowed by the magnificent Perpendicular church, built by Sir Michael de la Pole, the First Earl of Suffolk. Its great west tower is faced with freestone, and in a county of fine hammerbeam roofs, this church probably has the finest... complete with gloriously winged angels. There is a wonderful painted rood screen, fascinating misericords, a wooden 15th century pulpit, and as a foil for all these rich treasures, a floor of mellow tiles and bricks... all very satisfying.

2. Cawston Church

Salle
The splendid church of St. Peter and St. Paul stands by itself in unspoilt countryside, with its great 126 foot high tower dominating the landscape for miles around. It is without doubt the finest parish church in Norfolk, and is made doubly fascinating by its windy isolation, and the spacious solitude of its unspoilt interior. Endowed by three great families, the Boleyns, the Briggs and the Fountains, Salle has a wealth of splendours, both in its fabric and its furnishing, but see especially the west door, the two porches, the great font, its tall font cover suspended from a bracket on a high balcony, the stalls with their misericords, the medieval glass in the south transept and the multitude of interesting brasses.

3. Salle Church

Reepham
We found the town of Reepham to be full of character, with many 18th century, mellow brick houses gazing out over its little market square. There are no fewer than three churches in the combined churchyard... Hackford, a ruin since 1543, has only one wall surviving, but Reepham and Whitwell survive, and are most unusually joined, with a vestry common to both.

4. Reepham

Map 4

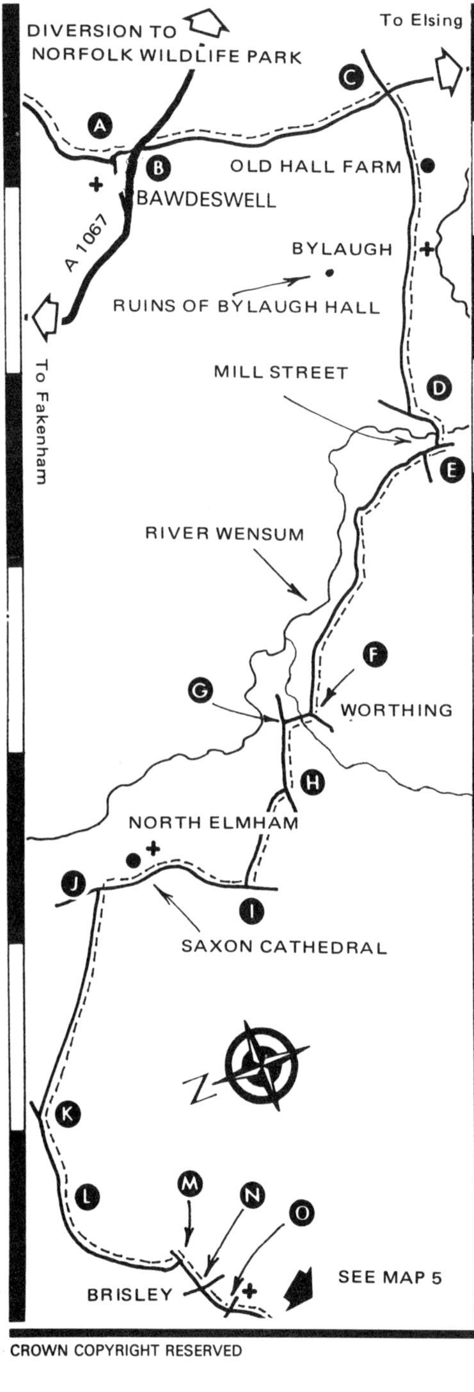

Directions — Sign-posted

	kms Ref. Miles	Directions	Sign-posted
	1.0	Entering Bawdeswell	
A	.1	Straight, not right (But turn right if you wish to visit church and village)	Norwich
	.2	Turn left, on to A1067, and... almost immediately...	Norwich
B	.1	Turn right, off A1067 (But go straight ahead on A1067 for about 4 miles if you wish to visit the Norfolk Wildlife Park)	Elsing
C	1.5	Turn right at X rds. by lodge (But if you wish to visit Elsing Church, go straight, then turn right at T junction, then over X rds... 1.2, but well worthwhile)	Bylaugh Church
	.4	Old Hall Farm on left (Pick up key if you wish to visit Bylaugh church)	
	.5	Bylaugh church on left	
D	.9	Turn left on to B1147	Dereham
	.3	Over two bridges crossing River Wensum, and...	
E		Turn right at T junction and...	Worthing
		Turn right at 2nd T junction	Worthing
	.2	Flooded gravel pits on right. (Day Fishing tickets available at farm by Point E)	
	.5	River Wensum alongside on right	
F	1.1	Turn right at T junction in Worthing Hamlet	North Elmham
	.1	Over stream	
G	.1	Turn left at T junction on to B1145, and... North Elmham entry signed	North Elmham
H	.3	Turn right at T junction beyond level crossing	No sign
I	.7	Turn right at T junction on to B1110	No sign
	.5	Church on right	
	.1	Cathedral ruins on right	
J	.3	Turn left at T junction	Gately
K	.3	Straight, not right	Brisley
	.5	Pleasant woodlands on right	
L	.5	Bear left at T junction	Brisley
M	.6	Bear left at T junction	Brisley
N	1.0	Turn right at T junction	No sign
O	.3	Over X rds., joining B1145, in Brisley (But turn left if you wish to visit church and village)	Mileham
		Total mileage on this map: 12.1	

CROWN COPYRIGHT RESERVED

On Route

Bawdeswell
Small village with an old-half-timbered building (Chaucer's House*) looking across the busy A1067 to the neo-Georgian church... built in 1955 to replace one destroyed in an aircraft accident. This is a handsome little building, and is elegantly furnished with gallery and three decker pulpit.
*Chaucer's Reeve hailed from Bawdeswell.

Norfolk Wildlife Park, Great Witchingham
Founded in 1962 by Philip Wayre, this was Britain's first Wildlife Park. It has the largest collection of European mammals and birds in the world, exhibited in natural surroundings. The emphasis is on conservation and captive breeding of endangered species. The Park's breeding successes with European mammals have never been equalled and include many 'firsts' in captivity in Britain.

Elsing
The diversion at Point C takes us past an attractive weatherboarded mill, to visit Elsing church. Here is probably the finest monumental brass in England (Sir Hugh Hastings 1347). It lies hidden beneath a plinth, supporting a fine glass fibre replica, which may itself be 'rubbed' for a fee. Apply to Mrs. Eileen Henley, 2, Church View, for both church key and/or permission to take a rubbing... it is well worthwhile. Do not overlook the handsome 14th century font cover.

Bylaugh Church
Its delightful setting on the banks of the Wensum is rather marred by the sewage works nearby. The church has a round tower with octagonal top, and inside there is a pleasing Georgian flavour with box pews and pulpit, all dating from a restoration carried out in 1810. See also the attractive brass of Sir John Curson, and his lady (1471). For key, see route directions. Bylaugh Hall is visible from our road, a ruined neo-Tudor mansion built in the 1850's by Charles Barry.

Mill Street, Swanton Morley
Here are quiet meadowlands with an old brick bridge spanning the Wensum, and beyond it, a handsome Georgian mill house.

North Elmham
Long, straggling and pleasantly sleepy village, which has the unusual distinction of possessing the remains of an Anglo-Saxon cathedral, once the seat of the Bishop of Norfolk (this bishopric was however finally settled upon Norwich in 1096). The ruins are intermingled with the remains of a fortified manor built by a Bishop of Norwich, and neither could be described as dramatic. However there are trees and grass, and old walls, and a flavour of the simplicity of early Christianity in England.

The nearby parish church has a fine tall tower, with an unusually shallow porch to the west door at its foot. The interior has been rather heavily restored, but its contents include a 17th century pulpit and a 15th century screen with interesting painted panels.

Brisley (See Page 11)

1. *At The Norfolk Wildlife Park*
Photograph by Patricia Wayre

2. *River Wensum, at Bylaugh*

3. *Bridge near Point E*

4. *North Elmham Cathedral*

Map 5

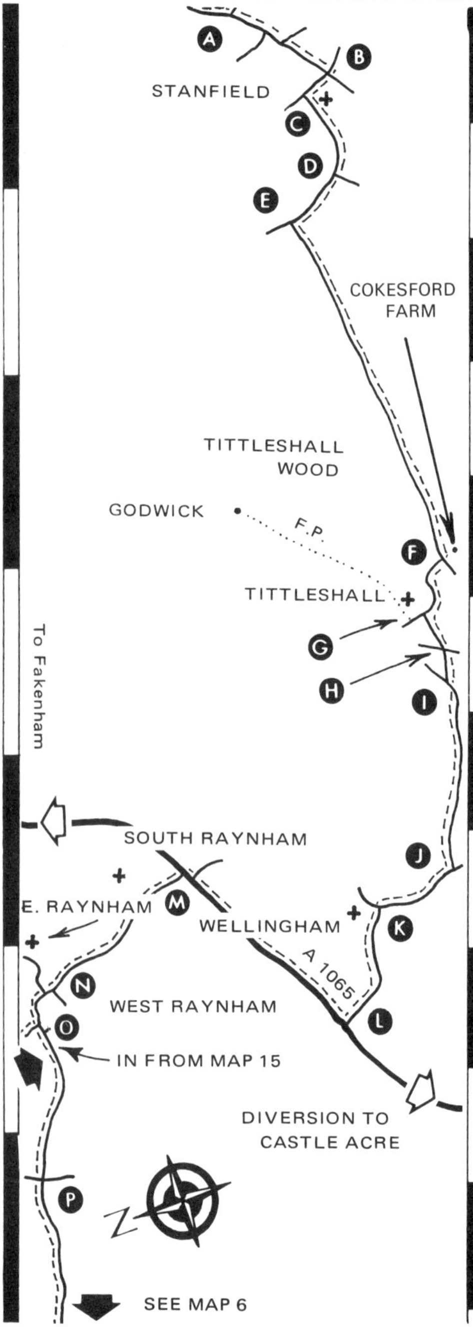

Ref.	kms/Miles	Directions	Sign-posted
A	.3	Straight, not left	No sign
	.1	Over offset X rds., crossing B1146	King's Lynn
B	.4	Turn right at offset X rds. off B1145	Whissonsett
C	.3	Turn left, by Stanfield church	Tittleshall
D	.4	Straight, not left	Tittleshall
E	.3	Turn left at T junction	Tittleshall
	1.1	Tittleshall Wood on right	
F	.8	Turn right at T junction	Fakenham
G	.3	Turn left by Tittleshall church	Weasenham
H	.2	Over offset, angled X rds.	Wellingham
I	.2	Straight, not right, at Y junction	No sign
J	.9	Turn right at T junction (Now at 265 feet above sea level)	Wellingham
K	.5	Turn left at T junction in Wellingham	Weasenham
	.1	Church on right	
L	.6	Turn right, on to A1065 (But turn left if you wish to visit Castle Acre, 6½ miles)	Cromer
M	1.4	Straight, not right, at entry to S. Raynham, and... Turn left, off A1065	Cromer / West Raynham
	.2	Roadway to church on right	
N	.7	Over X rds. at entry to West Raynham (But turn right if you wish to visit East Raynham church)	Helhoughton
	.1	Ruins of West Raynham church on right, close to the Greyhound Inn	
O	.1	Straight, not right	East Rudham
		(WE ARE JOINED HERE FROM THE END OF MAP 15)	
	.1	Straight, not left	No sign
	.5	Airfield visible over to left	
P	.2	Over X rds.	East Rudham
	.2	Beware of aircraft. Road close to runway at this point	
		Total mileage on this map: 10.0	

CROWN COPYRIGHT RESERVED

On Route

Brisley
The tall towered church is full of atmosphere and its contents include a three decker pulpit, an old box pew (dated 1590), a tall 15th century screen, fragments of medieval wall paintings, and an unusually attractive Victorian stained glass east window. Do not overlook the brass of a priest (1531) in the chancel floor.

Stanfield
The church is pleasantly set in a tree bordered churchyard, and its simple interior, although restored by the Victorians, is quite charming. Features of interest include a simple Jacobean font cover, like a little cage, poppy head bench ends embellished with animals and a two decker pulpit.

1. Stanfield Church

Tittleshall
An unexceptional village lying beyond extensive woodlands and open roads from which there are fine views southwards. Do not miss the church however, for inside will be found a series of splendid monuments by such renowned sculptors as Nicholas Stone, Atkinson, Nollekens and Roubiliac... all commemorating members of the Coke family, who lived at nearby Godwick Hall before moving northwards to the new grandeur of Holkham (See Page 21). Godwick is now only a fragmentary ruin, but it can be reached by a path over the fields from Tittleshall.

2. Coke Monument, Tittleshall

Wellingham
Set in a neat, well mown churchyard, Wellingham church contains one feature of outstanding interest... a 16th century rood screen with an unusually vivid series of paintings.

Castle Acre Diversion
This diversion of thirteen miles in all is more than justified by the features that Castle Acre has to offer. Most of the old village lies within the outer 'bailey' of the Norman castle (built by William de Warenne, 1st Earl of Surrey, soon after the Conquest), the massive earthworks of which dominate the little street running down to the river. At its upper end lies the Bailey Gate and beyond this a wide tree lined street leading to the parish church (see the font, font cover, misericords, and painted 15th century pulpit), and beyond it to the Priory. This Cluniac house was founded in about 1090 by the 2nd Earl. It has a beautiful west front to its church, to which is attached the attractive 16th century 'Prior's House'. There are also extensive remains of the monastic quarters, and the whole priory is delightfully sited in meadows just above the river, with chestnut trees and well mown lawns.

3. Castle Acre Priory

South Raynham
Its church has an unusual medieval altar slab (13th century?) and a rather pleasing east window, which we suspect, must be the work of the craftsman responsible for the Brisley window (see above).

West Raynham, Raynham Hall and East Raynham Church (See Page 13)

4. Raynham Hall

Map 6

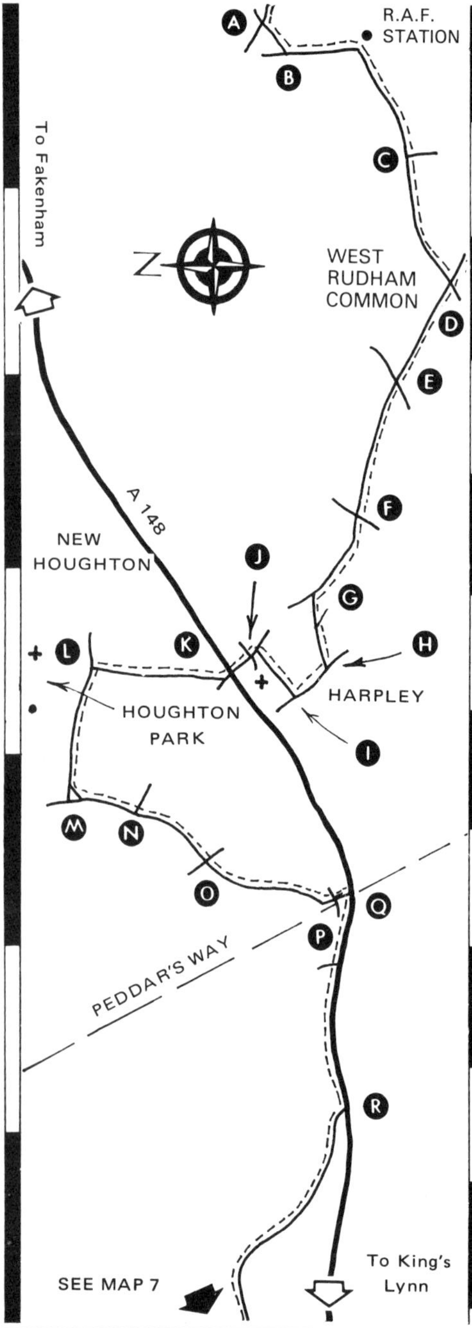

Ref	kms/Miles	Directions	Sign-posted
A	.5	Turn left at X rds.	Massingham
B	.2	Turn left at T junction	Massingham
	.4	Turn right (R.A.F. West Raynham on left)	Rougham
C	.6	Straight, not left	Harpley
D	.6	Turn right at X rds.	Harpley
E	.6	Over X rds by course of old railway	No sign
F	.7	Over open X rds.	No sign
G	.4	Turn left at T junction by cottages	No sign
	.1	Straight, not left, at Y junction	No sign
H	.3	Bear right, on to wider road	No sign
	.1	Rose & Crown Inn on right	
I	.1	Turn right at T junction by Harpley village sign	No sign
	.1	Harpley church on left	
J	.2	Turn left at T junction	No sign
	.1	Over X rds.	No sign
K	.1	Over X rds., crossing A148, and immediately.... Straight, not left, keeping on wider road Fine road with wide grass borders and avenue of trees	Houghton
L	.7	Turn left at T junction by gates of Houghton Park	Bircham
	.1	Houghton Hall visible over to right	
M	.5	Fork left	No sign
	.1	Straight, not right, twice	No sign
N	.3	Straight, not left	No sign
O	.4	Over small open X rds.	No sign
P	.7	Over small X rds. joining Peddar's Way for a short distance	No sign
Q	.1	Turn right, on to A148	No sign
		Peddar's Way crosses A148 at this point	
	.2	Straight, not right	
R	1.0	Turn right, off A148, opposite layby on left (WATCH FOR THIS WITH GREAT CARE)	No sign
		Total mileage on this map: 9.2	

CROWN COPYRIGHT RESERVED

12

On Route

West Raynham (See Page 10)
An undistinguished village with an uninteresting ivy covered ruin of a church close to the brick built Greyhound Inn.

Raynham Hall and East Raynham Church
(See Page 10)
Here beyond a noble avenue of trees, with a lake below, we can see the front of the beautiful 17th century mansion of Raynham Hall. This was almost certainly designed by William Edge, who had travelled to Holland with Sir Roger Townsend, the owner; and the charming gable ends are inescapable proof of Dutch influence. Here lived Sir Charles 'Turnip' Townsend, one of the leading figures of the 18th century 'Agrarian Revolution', and Sir Charles Townsend, who conducted the epic defence of Kut in the 1914 – 18 War.

The Townsend memorials, including a very grand Easter Sepulchre, are the chief items of interest in East Raynham church, which was re-built in 1868, and lies at the end of our diversion, close to the lake.

1. *On West Rudham Common*

Harpley
Pleasant unassuming village situated on rising ground, with a small inn, the Rose and Crown, and a tall towered church in a tree shaded churchyard. The church has an ambitious porch, sheltering a fine old door, with carved figures around it. The well proportioned interior contains some poppy head bench ends, embellished with animal carvings, but unfortunately the figures on the rood screen have been re-painted by the Victorians.

2. *Avenue to Houghton*

New Houghton and Houghton Hall
A splendid avenue of trees lines our road to New Houghton, a village built in 1729 to replace the village pulled down by Sir Robert Walpole to improve the view from his magnificent new mansion, Houghton Hall. This was designed by Colin Campbell for England's first Prime Minister, and is Norfolk's largest country seat. This is open to the public and contains a fine collection of furniture, pictures and porcelain. A far glimpse of the Hall may be obtained from our route a short distance beyond the white painted gates to the park.

3. *Gates to Houghton Park*

Peddar's Way
This is the name of a Roman road that ran in a N.N.W. direction, probably starting from Chelmsford, and certainly finishing near Holme-next-the-Sea (See page 17). Its function is not certain, but it is reasonable to suppose that there was a ferry service across the Wash to Burgh-le-Marsh in Lincolnshire, from whence a further Roman road ran north west. This pleasant mixture of by-road, bridle-way and footpath is now an official long distance footpath, running up through Castle Acre (page 11) to Holme-next-the-Sea (page 17), where it links with another newly designated long distance footpath, the Norfolk Coast Path, which runs eastwards from Holme to Cromer.

4. *Houghton Hall*

Map 7

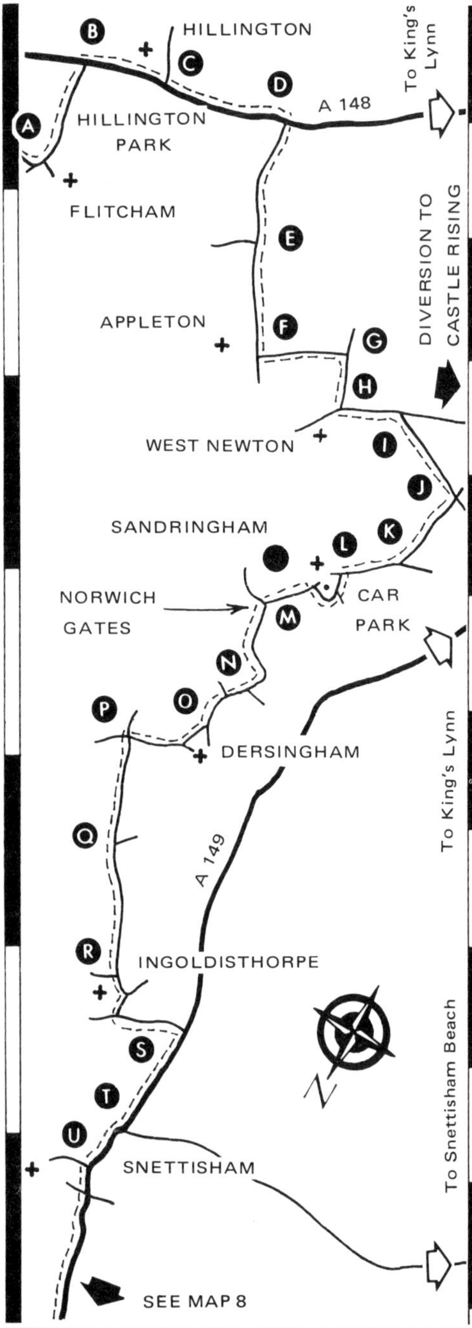

Directions / Signposted

Ref.	kms	Miles	Directions	Signposted
A	1.2	.3	Flitcham Abbey (farm) on left Bear left in Flitcham, by New Inn	No sign
		.1	Bear left again, by village sign (But go straight over if you wish to visit church)	No sign
		.5	Hillington entry signed	
B		.1	Turn right, on to A148	King's Lynn
C		.5	Straight, not left (But turn left, if you wish to visit church)	King's Lynn
D		.6	Turn right, on to B1440	Sandringham
E		.7	Straight, not right	No sign
F		.6	Turn left, off B1440 (Ruins of Appleton church up right)	No sign
G		.5	Turn right at T junction	No sign
		.2	Enter West Newton	
H		.1	Turn left at T junction by village sign (But turn right if you wish to visit church)	No sign
I		.3	Fork right. (But fork left if you wish to visit Castle Rising...2.4 miles) Open, bracken covered country	No sign
J		.6	Turn right at X rds. by Lynn Lodges	No sign
K		.5	Straight, not left at Y junction	No sign
L		.4	Bear left at T junction	'P'
		.1	Straight, not left, by large car park on right (For visitors to Sandringham church, etc.)	No sign
		.1	Turn left at T junction	No sign
M		.2	Turn left by Norwich Gates	King's Lynn
		.4	Dersingham entry signed	
N		.2	Bear right at Y junction keeping on wider road	No sign
		.1	Straight, not right, by Coach and Horses	No sign
O		.2	Fork right just before church	'Church Lane'
		.1	Turn right at T junction	No sign
P		.3	Turn left at X rds	'Mill Road'
Q		.6	Straight, not left	No sign
R		.8	Bear left at T junction in Ingoldisthorpe (But turn right if you wish to visit church)	No sign
		.1	Turn right at T junction	No sign
		.1	Turn left by hotel	No sign
S		.3	Turn right, on to A149	No sign
		.4	Snettisham entry signed	
T		.3	Keep straight through Snettisham on A149 (But turn left if you wish to visit beach)	Hunstanton
U		.3	Straight, not right by the Compasses Inn (But turn right if you wish to visit church) Follow out of Snettisham on A149 Total mileage on this map: 11.8	Hunstanton

SEE MAP 8

CROWN COPYRIGHT RESERVED

On Route

Flitcham
Attractive village on the edge of Hillington Park, with views of a lake from the churchyard.

Hillington
Has a stone built inn, the Ffolkes Arms, standing close to the park gates. Do not miss the interesting series of monuments in the church.

Appleton
The ivy clad ruins of a small 12th century round towered church stand beside a farm road.

1. West Newton Church

West Newton
Very much an estate village of Sandringham House with a strong Victorian and Edwardian flavour. The church stands in a neat churchyard, and although almost entirely re-built in 1881 (organ presented by Queen Victoria), it contains an octagonal font with a handsome 17th or 18th century Gothick font cover. Note the carved village sign at Point I. This is one of a series of attractively carved and coloured village signs in the area, most of which were presented by King George V.

Castle Rising Diversion
This diversion of five miles in all is justified by the splendid castle alone, but the Norman church and Trinity Hospital are also of great interest. The castle was built about 1150 and now consists of a great Norman keep surrounded by massive circular earth works. The church has a beautiful Norman west doorway and chancel arch, and a fine square Norman font. The Trinity Hospital is a range of mellow brick almshouses built in 1614 by Henry Howard, Earl of Northampton, for 'ten spinsters'. It is still blessed with its original furnishings, and is now occupied by spinsters or widows, who go to church in their traditional red cloaks and pointed hats.

2. Steps at Castle Rising   3. Sandringham Church

Sandringham
Victorian mansion built by Edward, Prince of Wales in 1870, and used ever since as a holiday home by the Royal Family. The attractive gardens are open to the public when no member of the family is in residence, and there is free access to much of the glorious woods and heathland, through which our route passes... oaks, silver birch, pines and rhododendrons. This is now designated as a Countryside Park. There is a large car park complete with shop, a short distance from Sandringham church, a place of great interest, although much restored by the Victorians.

4. Woodlands at Sandringham

Dersingham
A large village with a big scale church. This has fine clear windows in nave and clerestory, and a stout tower. Inside there is a beautifully carved oak chest (15th century?), and an attractive tomb chest of John Peel (1607).

Ingoldisthorpe
The church here is tucked away on the eastern side of the village, and is not of great interest to visitors.

Snettisham and Snettisham Beach
(See Page 17)

5. Dersingham Church

Map 8

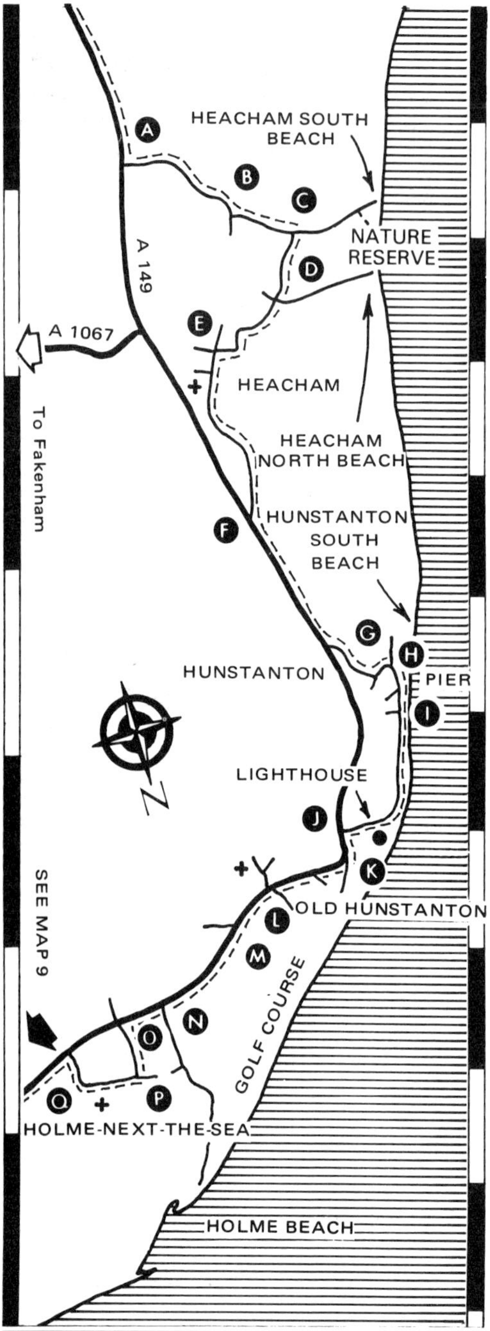

Ref.	kms / Miles	Directions	Sign-posted
A	1.2	Turn left at T junction, off A149	Heacham Beach
B	.8	Turn left at T junction	'The Beaches'
C	.4	Turn right (But go straight ahead if you wish to visit South Beach and/or Nature Reserve)	North Beach
D	.4	Over X rds. in Heacham (But turn left if you wish to visit North Beach)	No sign
	.1	Bear right at Y junction	No sign
E	.4	Turn left by the Wheatsheaf Inn	Hunstanton Road
	.2	Straight, not right, by church	No sign
F	1.0	Bear left on to A149	Hunstanton
	.3	Bear left on to B1161	South Beach
G	.6	Bear round to right at roundabout (But go straight ahead if you wish to visit South Beach)	Town Centre
H	.4	Straight, not right, by the Panama Leisure Bar	'Le Strange Terrace'
	.1	Car Parks on left	
I	.1	Straight, not right, by Green, keeping on sea front	No sign
	.7	Old Lighthouse on left, and	
		Straight, not left (But turn down left for good car parking area looking northwards over the sands)	No sign
J	.2	Turn left, on to A149	Wells
K	.2	Turn right, keeping on A149	Wells
L	.4	Over X rds. in Old Hunstanton, beyond the Neptune Hotel (But turn right if you wish to visit church)	No sign
M	.2	Fork left, keeping on A149	Wells
N	.7	Straight, not left, at entry to Holme (But turn left if you wish to visit Holme Beach)	No sign
O	.3	Turn left at X rds., off A149	No sign
P	.3	Turn right at T junction	No sign
	.1	White Horse Inn on left	
	.1	Church on left	
Q	.2	Turn left, rejoining A149	
		Total mileage on this map: 9.4	

CROWN COPYRIGHT RESERVED

On Route

Snettisham Beach (See Page 14)
Wide beach with a multitude of caravans and chalets behind its high shingle bank. Pebbles with sand at low tide. Excellent bird watching across the saltings, especially in winter time.

Snettisham (See Page 14)
Large sprawling village with several pleasant 18th century houses, and an attractive village sign. The church has a tall tower and spire with flying buttresses. Despite the loss of its chancel, it still remains a fine large church with a magnificently traceried west window and tall graceful arcading. See especially the monument to Sir Wymond Carye (1612).

Heacham — North and South Beach
Like Snettisham these beaches have vast caravan parks behind the high sea wall.

Heacham
Another large village with no special features apart from its neo-Tudor mill, which is now used for the manufacture of Norfolk lavender water (not on our route), and its 13th century church. This is prettily situated in trees, opposite an attractive group of cottages, and has a broad spacious interior, which includes amongst its contents, a handsome canopied monument to Robert Redmayne. There is also a modern monument in alabaster to Princess Pocohontas, the daughter of a Red Indian chief, who married local landowner John Rolfe in 1614.

Hunstanton
'New' Hunstanton was developed by the Le Strange family of Hunstanton Hall, upon the arrival of the railway in 1862. The whole town has an orderly, tidy appearance, with several pleasant stone buildings looking out over a wide green. There is an excellent sandy beach, overlooked at its northern end by Hunstanton's famous striped cliffs, upon which stand an old lighthouse and the fragmentary ruins of a Medieval chapel.

Old Hunstanton
The church is beautifully sited beyond flower decked cottages and a lively duck pond. It has a lofty interior, considerably restored in 1857, but do not miss the very fine brass to Sir Roger Le Strange (1506) on a tomb chest. Old Hunstanton also has a long sandy beach, lying beyond one of East Anglia's finest golf courses.

Holme-next-the-Sea
The Roman road, Peddar's Way (now a long distance footpath, which joins the Norfolk Coast Path here — see page 1), ended here, but no trace has yet been found of the small ferry port that it probably served. There are wide sands backed by dunes, much of which are within a Nature Reserve. For details write to the Warden, The Firs, Holme-next-the-Sea, Hunstanton, or phone Holme (048-525) 240.

Holme village is a quiet place with pleasant flower filled cottage gardens, a character inn, and a church with a 15th century brass and a pleasant 17th century wall monument in alabaster, with husband and wife facing each other at a prayer desk.

1. Cottages at Heacham

2. Cliffs at Hunstanton

3. Porch, Hunstanton

4. Font, Hunstanton

5. In Holme Churchyard

Map 9

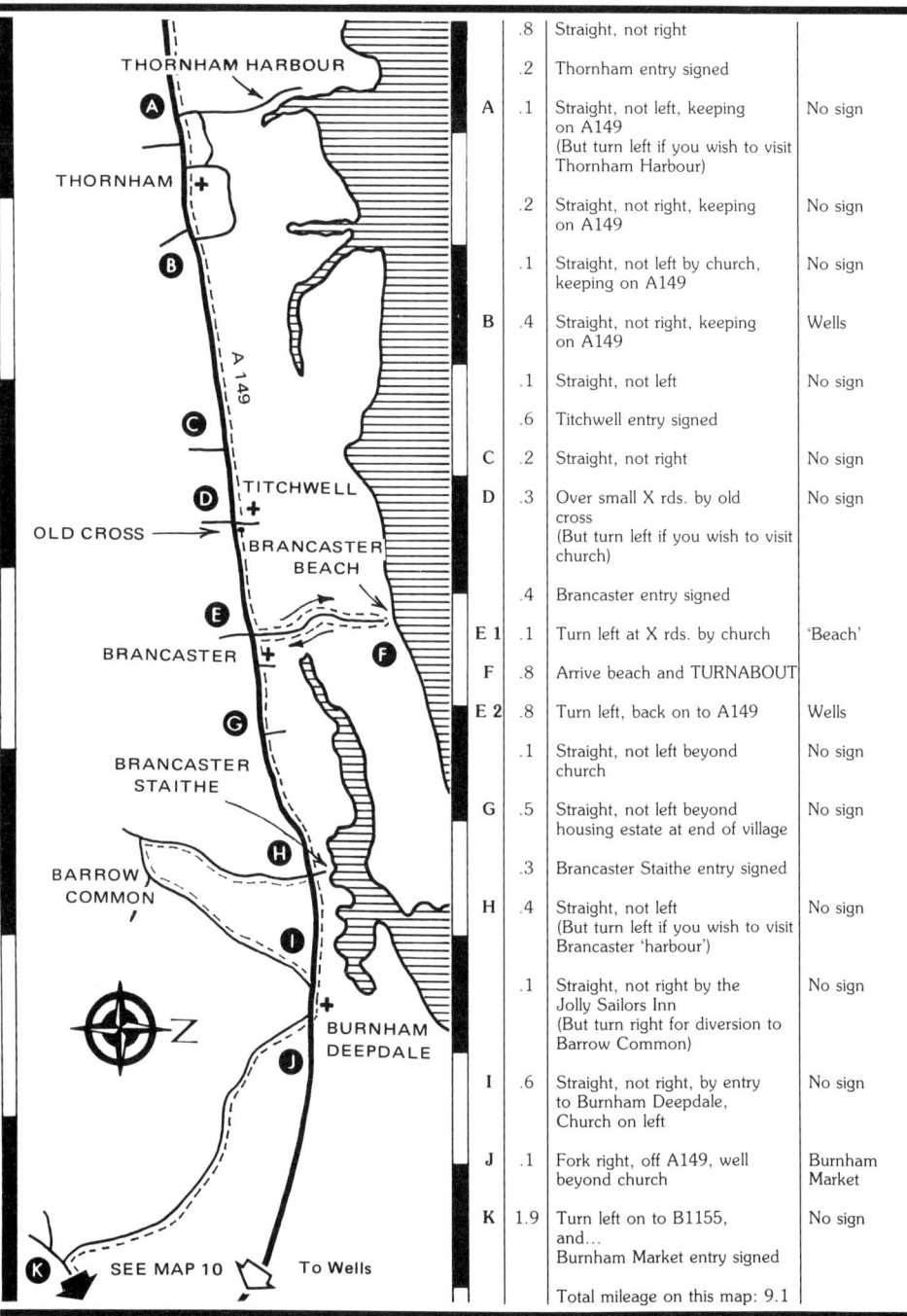

Ref.	kms/Miles	Directions	Sign-posted
	.8	Straight, not right	
	.2	Thornham entry signed	
A	.1	Straight, not left, keeping on A149 (But turn left if you wish to visit Thornham Harbour)	No sign
	.2	Straight, not right, keeping on A149	No sign
	.1	Straight, not left by church, keeping on A149	No sign
B	.4	Straight, not right, keeping on A149	Wells
	.1	Straight, not left	No sign
	.6	Titchwell entry signed	
C	.2	Straight, not right	No sign
D	.3	Over small X rds. by old cross (But turn left if you wish to visit church)	No sign
	.4	Brancaster entry signed	
E 1	.1	Turn left at X rds. by church	'Beach'
F	.8	Arrive beach and TURNABOUT	
E 2	.8	Turn left, back on to A149	Wells
	.1	Straight, not left beyond church	No sign
G	.5	Straight, not left beyond housing estate at end of village	No sign
	.3	Brancaster Staithe entry signed	
H	.4	Straight, not left (But turn left if you wish to visit Brancaster 'harbour')	No sign
	.1	Straight, not right by the Jolly Sailors Inn (But turn right for diversion to Barrow Common)	No sign
I	.6	Straight, not right, by entry to Burnham Deepdale, Church on left	No sign
J	.1	Fork right, off A149, well beyond church	Burnham Market
K	1.9	Turn left on to B1155, and... Burnham Market entry signed	No sign
		Total mileage on this map: 9.1	

CROWN COPYRIGHT RESERVED

On Route

Thornham
Pleasant village with pantiled cottages of chalk and flint grouped around its handsome church. This has an attractive two storeyed porch and a lofty nave with fine hammerbeam roof. See especially the octagonal font with painted heraldry, the Jacobean pulpit, and the fascinating series of carved bench ends (windmill, merman, dragon, etc.).

To the north of the village there are the remains of a small harbour on marshy Thornham Creek... all very atmospheric. Turn left at Point A. Excellent bird watching.

1. Thornham Harbour

Titchwell
Minute windswept village on the edge of the marshes, with a plain medieval cross at our turn down to the church. This has a Norman round tower, topped by a pretty little lead spire (adorned by a solitary and rather somnolent gull when we called here last). Inside the church there is an old tiled floor, a large Norman tub font and rows of ugly Victorian pews.

Brancaster
Small village with no special features apart from its church. This has a pleasant old south doorway leading to a light airy interior, with white plastered walls and much plain glass. See especially the carved wooden figure of a priest, the tall, pinnacled font cover, and the three handsome Italian lanterns. The site of the Roman town of BRANODONUM lies to the left of our road at the far end of the village, but there is little of real interest to be seen.

2. Ship Sign, Brancaster

Brancaster Beach
Reached by a pleasant winding road over the marshes, the wide sandy beach (dangerous for bathing at all times) is backed by a golf course behind the dunes. It is possible to walk eastwards (about 1½ miles) along the dunes to look across a channel to Scolt Head Island (see below).

Brancaster Staithe
A muddy little harbour, full of flavour, with one or two mellow brick houses, and many small boats drawn up on the shore. This is the departure point for boats to Scolt Head Island, which is a paradise for bird watchers, and all lovers of the solitary atmosphere of creeks and saltings. All in the care of the National Trust.

3. At Brancaster Staithe

Barrow Common
To visit this pleasant piece of common land, with gorse and bracken, and woodlands in the valley beyond, turn right by the Jolly Sailors Inn at Brancaster Staithe (beyond Point H), drive up to the common, then turn left twice beyond it, and rejoin the main route at Point I in Burnham Deepdale.

Burnham Deepdale
Here is a church with an Anglo-Saxon round tower and an exceptionally fine Norman font, with sculptured figures depicting the twelve 'Labours of the Months'. Do not miss this most satisfying illustration of life and work in medieval England.

4. Font, Burnham Deepdale

Map 10

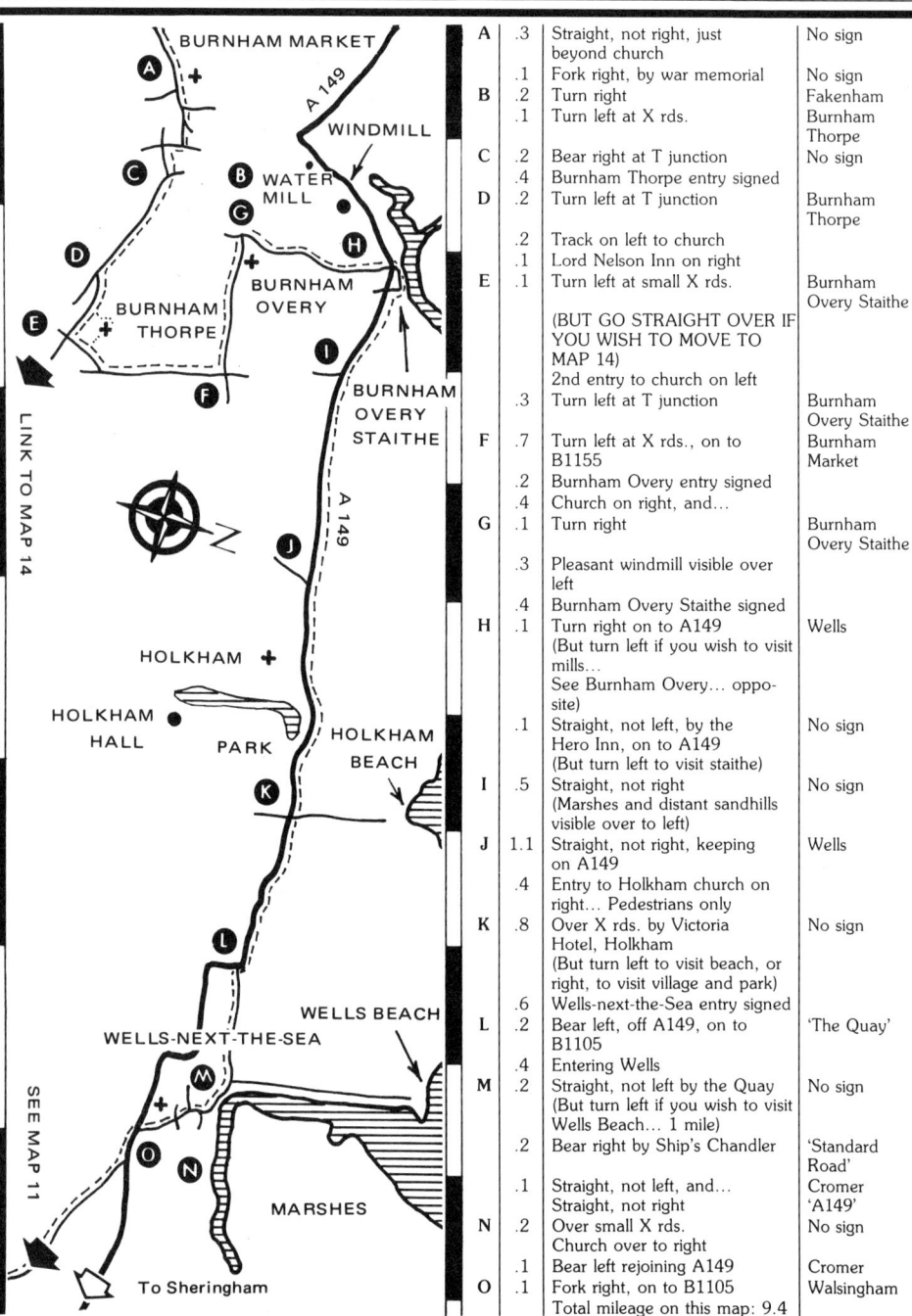

Ref.	kms / Miles	Directions	Sign-posted
A	.3	Straight, not right, just beyond church	No sign
	.1	Fork right, by war memorial	No sign
B	.2	Turn right	Fakenham
	.1	Turn left at X rds.	Burnham Thorpe
C	.2	Bear right at T junction	No sign
	.4	Burnham Thorpe entry signed	
D	.2	Turn left at T junction	Burnham Thorpe
	.2	Track on left to church	
	.1	Lord Nelson Inn on right	
E	.1	Turn left at small X rds. (BUT GO STRAIGHT OVER IF YOU WISH TO MOVE TO MAP 14) 2nd entry to church on left	Burnham Overy Staithe
	.3	Turn left at T junction	Burnham Overy Staithe
F	.7	Turn left at X rds., on to B1155	Burnham Market
	.2	Burnham Overy entry signed	
	.4	Church on right, and...	
G	.1	Turn right	Burnham Overy Staithe
	.3	Pleasant windmill visible over left	
	.4	Burnham Overy Staithe signed	
H	.1	Turn right on to A149 (But turn left if you wish to visit mills... See Burnham Overy... opposite)	Wells
	.1	Straight, not left, by the Hero Inn, on to A149 (But turn left to visit staithe)	No sign
I	.5	Straight, not right (Marshes and distant sandhills visible over to left)	No sign
J	1.1	Straight, not right, keeping on A149	Wells
	.4	Entry to Holkham church on right... Pedestrians only	
K	.8	Over X rds. by Victoria Hotel, Holkham (But turn left to visit beach, or right, to visit village and park)	No sign
	.6	Wells-next-the-Sea entry signed	
L	.2	Bear left, off A149, on to B1105	'The Quay'
	.4	Entering Wells	
M	.2	Straight, not left by the Quay (But turn left if you wish to visit Wells Beach... 1 mile)	No sign
	.2	Bear right by Ship's Chandler	'Standard Road'
	.1	Straight, not left, and... Straight, not right	Cromer 'A149'
N	.2	Over small X rds. Church over to right	No sign
	.1	Bear left rejoining A149	Cromer
O	.1	Fork right, on to B1105 Total mileage on this map: 9.4	Walsingham

CROWN COPYRIGHT RESERVED

On Route

Burnham Market
Has a delightful wide street with many Georgian houses, shops and inns, looking out across broad greens. The church has sculptured figures upon its tower battlements, but the interior is less interesting than many others on our route.

Burnham Thorpe
Horatio Nelson was born here in 1758, the fifth son of the Rev. Edmund Nelson. The parsonage was demolished long ago, but its site is marked by a plaque nearby (turn right at Point E, as the site lies off the route). However the church contains several more tangible reminders... a bust of Nelson to commemorate the centenary of his death, a plaque to Edmund Nelson, who died in 1789, and a crest from H.M.S. Nelson.

Burnham Overy
The church has a Norman tower topped by an attractive 17th century cupola. Our route misses the interesting windmill and watermill, and you should turn left at Point H if you wish to visit them.

Burnham Overy Staithe
Here is an old harbour on a muddy creek well up from the sea, overlooked by a mellow brick warehouse. Walk northwards to the dunes of Gun Hill for superlative bird watching.

Holkham Church
Walk from the road (See Route Directions) to this largely re-built church sited on a mound in heavily wooded Holkham Park. Inside all is gaunt and lonely, but there are two pleasing 17th century monuments, both by Nicholas Stone.

Holkham Hall
Magnificent Palladian mansion designed largely by William Kent, for Thomas Coke, descendant of Lord Chief Justice Coke (See Tittleshall, Page 11), and known as 'Coke of Norfolk', one of the leaders of the Agrarian Revolution. The proportions and colouring of the entrance hall and the saloon are outstanding, but the splendour of Holkham's decoration, furnishings and pictures cannot be adequately described in the space available here. The extensive park, with its long lake, and fine trees, may be walked through on Saturdays, Sundays and Bank Holidays.

Holkham
At the entrance to the park is a small estate village, complete with pottery, gift shop, and pleasant small hotel, the Victoria Arms. The beach, with its fabulously wide stretches of sand at low tide, is approached by an estate toll road.

Wells-next-the-Sea
Still has an active little quay, with narrow streets leading down to it from the Buttlands, a pleasant tree lined, open space overlooked by 18th century houses. The old warehouses on the quay look down towards the mouth of the estuary where there is a lifeboat station and a magnificent sandy beach backed by high dunes.

1. Burnham Overy Staithe

2. At Burnham Overy

3. At Burnham Market

4. Church and Inn, Burnham Thorpe

5. Bust of Nelson Burnham Thorpe

6. Holkham Hall   Photograph by Jarrold & Sons Ltd.

21

Map 11

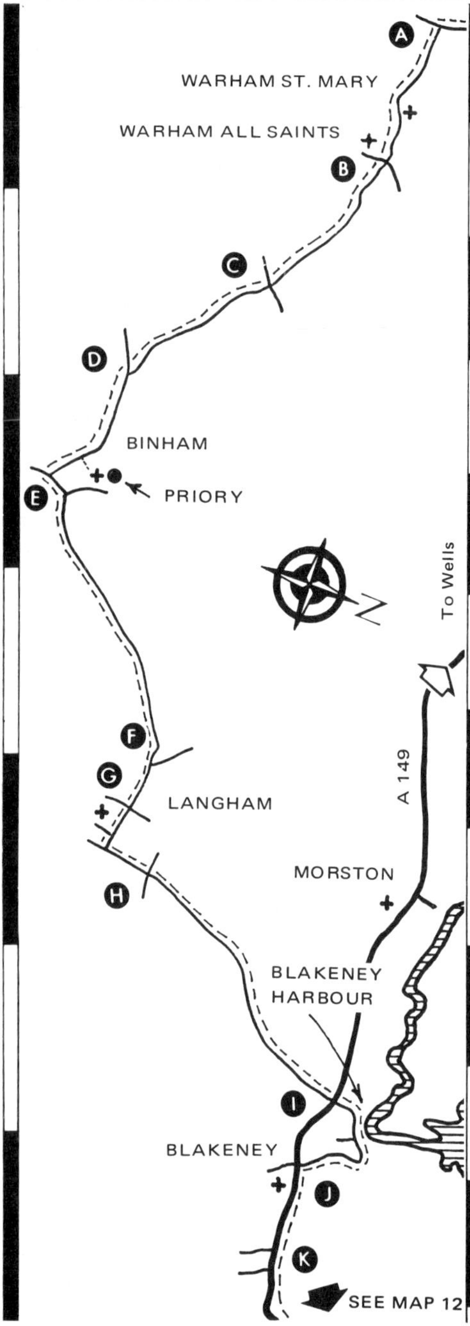

Ref.	kms / Miles	Directions	Sign-posted
A	1.1	Turn left at T junction, off B1105	Warham
	.4	Warham St. Mary church on left	
B	.4	Over X rds. by the Horseshoes Inn (But turn right if you wish to look at Warham All Saints Church)	Binham
C	.8	Over X rds.	Binham
D	.9	Bear left at Y junction	Binham
	.5	Entry to Binham church and priory ruins on left	
	.2	Turn sharp left on to B1388	Langham
	.1	Turn right at T junction, keeping on B1388	Langham
	1.4	Langham entry signed	
F	.2	Straight, not left at Y junction	Blakeney
G	.2	Over X rds. by Langham church	Holt
	.1	Straight, not right	No sign
	.1	Turn left at T junction, keeping on B1388	Blakeney
H	.3	Over X rds.	Blakeney
	1.3	Entering Blakeney	
I	.2	Over X rds., crossing A149 (But turn left if you wish to visit Morston)	Blakeney Quay
	.1	Quay on left	
	.1	Straight, not right, by Blakeney Hotel	No sign
J	.4	Turn left at X rds., rejoining A149	Holt
	.1	Blakeney church on right	
K	.4	Straight, not right, twice	Cley
		Total mileage on this map: 9.3	

CROWN COPYRIGHT RESERVED

On Route

Warham St. Mary Church
Although it has Norman origins, its interior has a pleasing late 18th century flavour, with box pews, altar rail and magnificent three decker pulpit. The attractive stained glass was inserted by a rector in the 1800's, and is probably Flemish.

Warham All Saints Church
This small building has a Norman font, a small brass (1474), and an elaborately carved reredos in alabaster representing the Last Supper.

Binham Priory and Church
The attractive ruins of Binham Priory, a Benedictine house established in 1091, incorporate the parish church of Binham (this was originally the nave of the Priory church). The church is mainly Norman, although the west front is 'Early English', and probably one of the very first examples of this style. However the Norman work in the interior is really splendid, especially when measured against its quiet setting in the remote Norfolk countryside. See especially the fine 'Seven Sacrament' font, and the two misericords beneath the choir stalls.

The ruins of the chancel and the adjoining monastic quarters are delightfully situated, and with the help of the plan displayed in the church one can obtain an excellent impression of the Priory as it must have been before the 'Dissolution' of 1540.

Binham
Pleasant flint village with a medieval cross on a little green, overlooked by the Chequers Inn and several attractive cottages.

Langham
Small village with a Perpendicular church, whose best feature is its tall west tower. Do not miss a visit to the Langham Glass House in North Street, where a team of glass-makers may usually be seen at work.

Morston Quay
Small, very basic quay on a tidal creek, in the salt marshes behind the Blakeney Channel.

Blakeney
Minute brick and flint town, full of character, with a narrow high street of bright little shops and inns leading down towards the old 'Guildhall' (with a 15th century brick built under-croft), and the famous quay. This is one of Norfolk's most attractive spots, with mellow brick buildings looking out over the saltings towards Blakeney Point, a shingle spit of 1100 acres owned by the National Trust, which is yet another paradise for bird watchers and naturalists. (Boats leave the quay for Blakeney Point regularly).

Blakeney church is an ambitious building with a fine Perpendicular tower and nave... all on a big scale. However the chancel is much smaller and much older, with low rib vaulting in the Early English style. Attached to the chancel is an unusual tower, thought to have been used as a beacon by those navigating up the difficult Blakeney Channel.

1. Binham Priory

2. Binham Priory   3. Warham St. Mary

4. Morston Quay

5. Blakeney Quay

Map 12

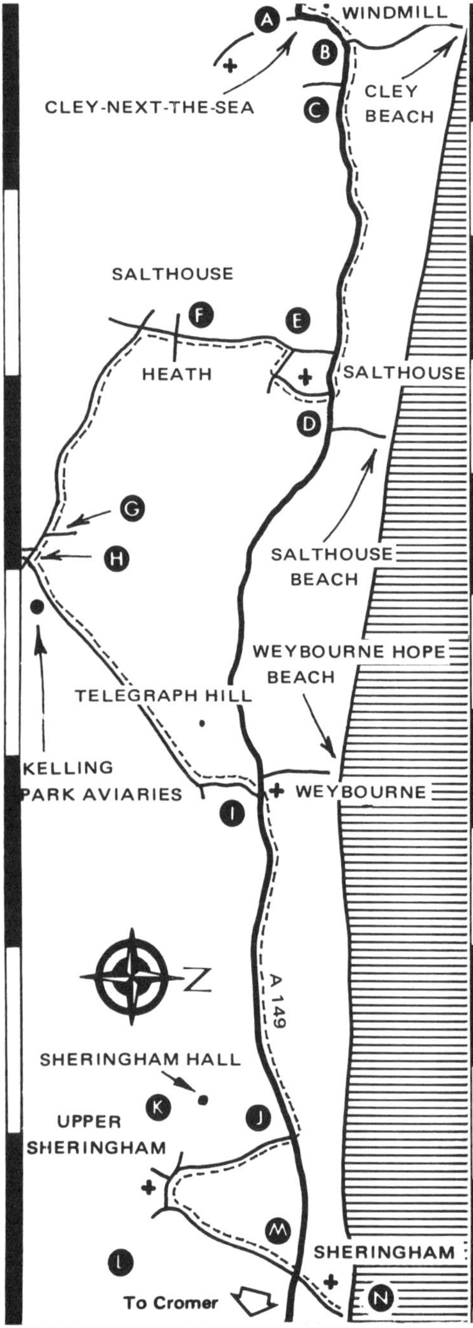

Ref	Miles	Directions	Signposted
A	.1	Cley entry signed	
	.2	Turn sharp left, keeping on A149 (But turn right if you wish to visit church)	Cromer
B	.1	Windmill over to left	
	.2	Straight, not left (But turn left if you wish to visit Cley Beach)	No sign
C	.3	Straight, not right, keeping on A149	Cromer
	1.3	Salthouse entry signed	
	.1	Bear left, keeping on A149, by the Dun Cow Inn	Cromer
D	.1	Turn right, off A149 (But go straight ahead, and first left if you wish to visit Salthouse Beach)	Cross Street
	.2	Church up to right	
	.2	Turn sharp right at T junction	No sign
E	.2	Turn sharp left at T junction	No sign
	.3	Climb up into Salthouse Heath area	
F	.4	Over X rds.	Holt
	.1	Turn left at X rds.	Bodham
G	1.2	Bear right at Y junction	High Kelling
	.1	Straight, not right, and...	High Kelling
H	.1	Turn left at X rds. (WE ARE JOINED HERE FROM THE END OF MAP 15)	Weybourne
	.2	Kelling Park Aviaries on right	
	.4	Now on Kelling Heath	
	1.0	Enter Weybourne	
	.2	Bear left at T junction	Kelling
I	.1	Turn right, on to A149, by Weybourne church (But turn left and almost immediately right if you wish to visit Weybourne Hope Beach)	Sheringham
J	1.7	Turn right at T junction off A149	Upper Sheringham
K	.7	Bear left, and... (Entry to Sheringham Hall up to right)	No sign
		Straight, not right	Sheringham
	.1	Upper Sheringham church on right	
L	.1	Turn left at T junction	Sheringham
	.3	Sheringham entry signed	
M	.5	Over X rds., crossing A149 (Keep straight in towards Town Centre and Sea Front)	'Town Centre'
N	.4	Arrive Sheringham Sea Front, by the Crown Inn (THIS LINKS WITH MAP 1, POINT A)	
		Total mileage on this map: 10.9	

CROWN COPYRIGHT RESERVED

On Route

Cley-next-the-Sea
In medieval times Cley was a seaport town on the now reclaimed Glaven estuary, and the splendid 14th century church (do not miss the lovely south porch, the font and the many brasses) must have looked out over busy quays. The tidal Glaven still sweeps up beside Cley's beautiful windmill, and there are many attractive 18th century houses of brick and flint in the busy narrow street.

Cley and Salthouse Beaches and Marshes
There are access roads to both these beaches, which are backed by high shingle banks. The marshes between the sea and the main road present outstanding opportunities for bird watchers, and permits are available from the Visitor Centre, which is open from April to October, from 10 – 5 (but closed on Mondays, except Bank Holiday Mondays).

Salthouse
Small village sloping down to the edge of marsh meadows, bordered here by a winding channel, known as 'The Skirts', with geese and ducks in abundance. Until these meadows were created by drainage in the 17th century, Salthouse was a small port, linked to Cley's Glaven estuary. Salthouse church lies above the village and was largely built by Sir Henry Heydon of Baconsthorpe Castle, in the reign of Henry VII. Its interior is simple and unspoilt by over-restoration, with fine roofs, old tile and brick floors, and much plain glass.

Kelling Park Hotel and Aviaries
Attractively situated close to Kelling Heath, with an outstanding collection of tropical birds, the collection of Lories and Lorikeet being considered one of the finest in Europe. See also the flamingoes, cranes, cockatoos, macaws, toucans and black swans.

Kelling Heath
Open country with gorse and bracken, with views of pine woods to the south and east, and views of Weybourne from Telegraph Hill.

Weybourne
The shingly beach is overlooked by low cliffs, with erosion very much in evidence. We have happy memories of Weybourne, with its flint cottages, tall church and priory ruins close by, as we made the hospitable Maltings Hotel our base during several Norfolk visits. Weybourne Station is the present western terminus of the North Norfolk Railway (See Sheringham, page 3).

Upper Sheringham
A quiet place beneath wooded hills, with cottages and church overlooking a quaint 19th century well head 'reservoir'. Inside the church there is a 15th century rood screen complete with loft, and a handsome monument to Abbot Upcher (1819), for whom Sheringham Hall was built by Humphrey Repton. Now owned by the National Trust, it stands in a fine park, parts of which are open to the public at rhododendron time (see inside rear cover for times).

1. Cley Windmill   2. South Porch, Cley

3. Font, Cley

4. Cley Bird Sanctuary

5. The Maltings Hotel, Weybourne

Map 13

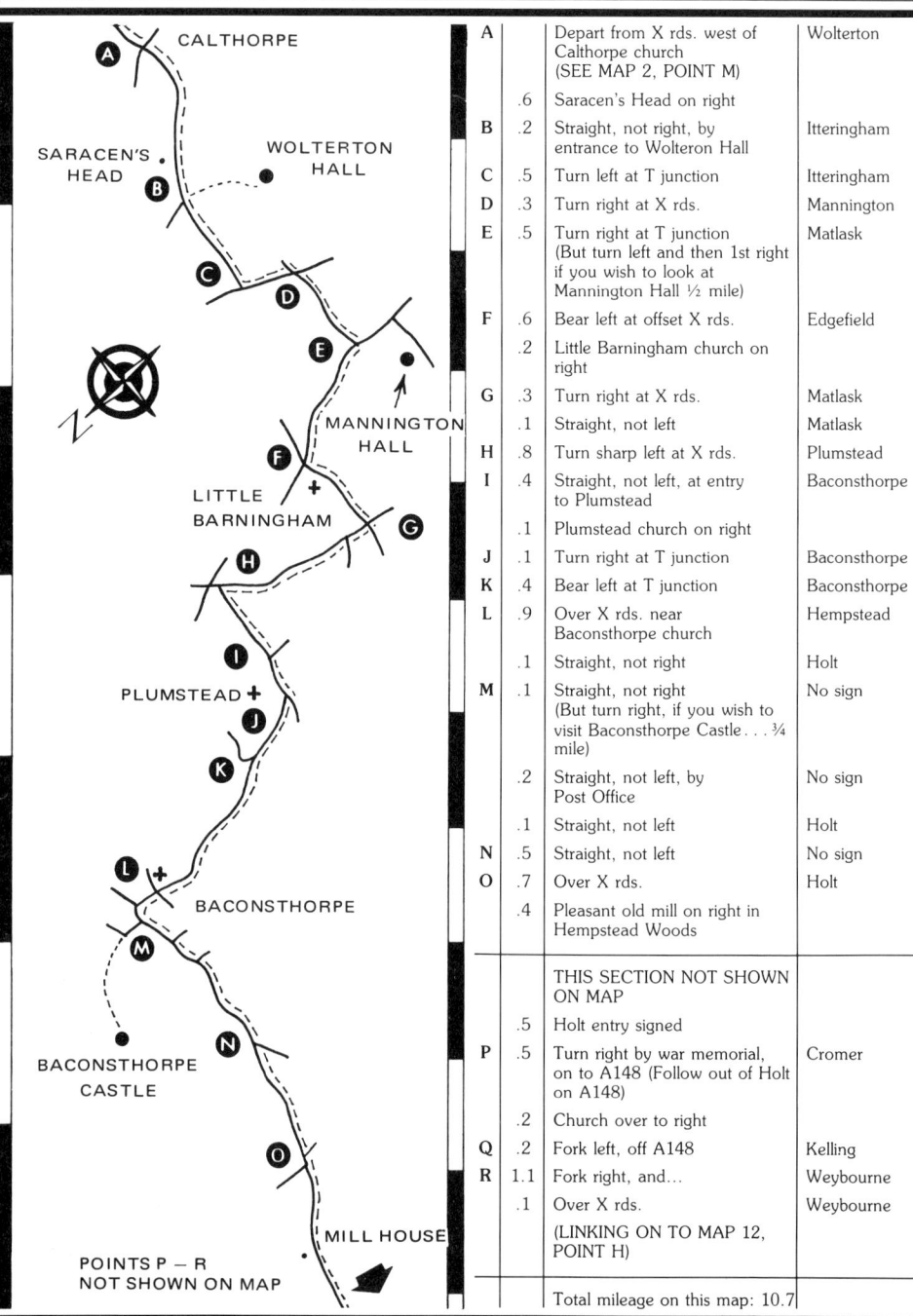

Ref.	kms / Miles	Directions	Sign-posted
A		Depart from X rds. west of Calthorpe church (SEE MAP 2, POINT M)	Wolterton
	.6	Saracen's Head on right	
B	.2	Straight, not right, by entrance to Wolterton Hall	Itteringham
C	.5	Turn left at T junction	Itteringham
D	.3	Turn right at X rds.	Mannington
E	.5	Turn right at T junction (But turn left and turn 1st right if you wish to look at Mannington Hall ½ mile)	Matlask
F	.6	Bear left at offset X rds.	Edgefield
	.2	Little Barningham church on right	
G	.3	Turn right at X rds.	Matlask
	.1	Straight, not left	Matlask
H	.8	Turn sharp left at X rds.	Plumstead
I	.4	Straight, not left, at entry to Plumstead	Baconsthorpe
	.1	Plumstead church on right	
J	.1	Turn right at T junction	Baconsthorpe
K	.4	Bear left at T junction	Baconsthorpe
L	.9	Over X rds. near Baconsthorpe church	Hempstead
	.1	Straight, not right	Holt
M	.1	Straight, not right (But turn right, if you wish to visit Baconsthorpe Castle...¾ mile)	No sign
	.2	Straight, not left, by Post Office	No sign
	.1	Straight, not left	Holt
N	.5	Straight, not left	No sign
O	.7	Over X rds.	Holt
	.4	Pleasant old mill on right in Hempstead Woods	
		THIS SECTION NOT SHOWN ON MAP	
	.5	Holt entry signed	
P	.5	Turn right by war memorial, on to A148 (Follow out of Holt on A148)	Cromer
	.2	Church over to right	
Q	.2	Fork left, off A148	Kelling
R	1.1	Fork right, and...	Weybourne
	.1	Over X rds. (LINKING ON TO MAP 12, POINT H)	Weybourne
		Total mileage on this map: 10.7	

CROWN COPYRIGHT RESERVED

On Route

Wolterton Hall
18th century mansion, built by Sir Robert Walpole's (See Houghton, Page 13) brother, Horatio Walpole. It was designed by Thomas Ripley, who appears to have worked at Houghton with Colin Campbell. The house is just visible to the left of our road immediately before reaching Point C, but it is not open to the public.

Mannington Hall
Another Walpole family property, this 15th century moated manor house is beautifully set in wooded gardens*, with a small lake. The interior of the house is full of atmosphere, and a visit here is well worth the trouble of making an appointment in advance.
*No appointment necessary for gardens. See inside rear cover.

Little Barningham
The village is not in any way exceptional, apart from the siting of its small Perpendicular church. This stands high above our road and has a 17th century pew, intended only for 'couples in wedlock'... it is cheerfully inscribed...
    'As you are now, even so was I,
    Remember death, for ye must dye'...
and for further comfort has a shrouded skeleton on one of the corner posts.

Plumstead
Stands on a slight rise and is rather more attractive than Little Barningham. We liked the neat, well tended churchyard and the coat of arms in memory of George VI and the attractive fragments of 15th century glass in the east window.

Baconsthorpe
In the village there is a pleasant old manor house, a Georgian rectory, and a church with an interior full of interest. See especially the fine alabaster wall monument to Sir William Heydon and his wife, with two figures, not facing each other, but both facing southwards, looking out of the window into the sunlight.
About a mile to the north west of the village, standing in quiet farmland, are the interesting ruins of Baconsthorpe Castle, built by Sir Henry Heydon, Recorder of Norwich in 1486. Some walls, towers, and a gatehouse remain from the original castle, the Hall being a 16th century conversion of an outer gatehouse.

Holt
A pleasant market town with a wealth of colourful Georgian buildings, for which we have a disastrous fire in 1708 to thank. This fire also gutted the church, and thanks to this and to the Victorian 'restorer' Butterfield, it is not of outstanding interest to visitors. Gresham School, founded by City merchant, John Gresham in 1555, when Lord Mayor, continues to flourish, but it is now situated to the north east of the town.

1. Baconsthorpe Churchyard

2. Baconsthorpe Castle

3. Baconsthorpe Castle   4. At Holt

5. Beyond Kelling Heath, near Weybourne (see page 25)

Map 14

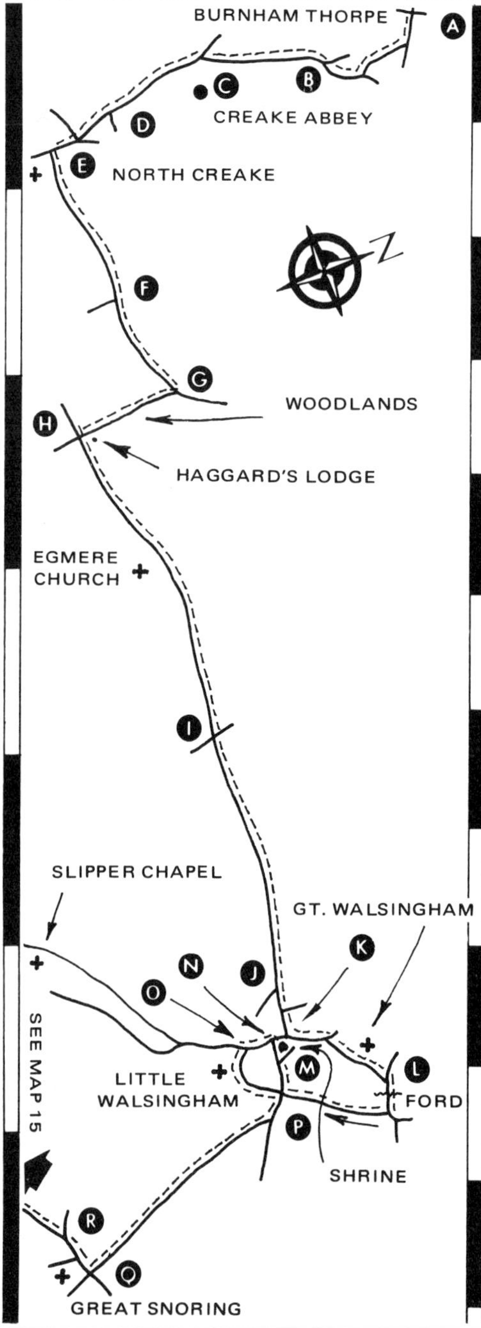

Ref	Miles	Directions	Sign-posted
A		Depart from Burnham Thorpe, by going straight over X rds. (SEE MAP 10, POINT E)	'Walsingham Rd'
	.1	Methodist Church on right	
	.2	Turn right at X rds.	Fakenham
B	.4	Bear left, on to wider road	Fakenham
C	.7	Bear left, on to B1355 (But turn full left if you wish to visit Creake Abbey)	Fakenham
	.3	North Creake entry signed	
D	.2	Straight, not left at T junction	No sign
	.2	Over X rds., by the Jolly Farmers Inn	Fakenham
E	.2	Turn left at T junction by Post Office (But go straight ahead if you wish to visit church)	No sign
F	1.0	Straight, not right, at T junction	No sign
G	.4	Turn sharp right in pleasant woodlands	Fakenham
H	.6	Turn left at X rds., at Haggards Lodge	Walsingham
	1.1	Ruins of Egmere church over to right	
I	.7	Over X rds.	Walsingham
J	1.2	Straight, not right	No sign
	.1	Straight, not left	Walsingham
	.1	Enter Little Walsingham	
K	.1	Bear left at T junction, and... Bear left by war memorial	No sign Wighton
	.2	Turn right	'Unbridged Ford'
	.2	Great Walsingham church on left	
L	.1	Bear right by green	No sign
	.1	Through ford	
K	.1	Turn right	'To the Shrine'
M 1	.5	Turn right at X rds.	Wells
	.2	Straight, not right by Shrine	Houghton
N	.1	Turn left by conduit, and... Straight, not right	No sign Houghton
O	.1	Bear left at X rds. (But go straight ahead if you wish to visit the Slipper Chapel at Houghton... 1.2 miles)	No sign
	.1	Little Walsingham church on right	
M 2	.3	Turn right at X rds.	Gt. Snoring
P	.2	Fork right	Gt. Snoring
Q	1.1	Turn right at X rds. in Great Snoring (But go over X rds. if you wish to visit church)	East Barsham
	.1	Straight, not left	East Barsham
R	.1	Fork left	East Barsham
		Total mileage on this map: 11.1	

CROWN COPYRIGHT RESERVED

28

On Route

Creake Abbey
Ruined 13th century Augustinian abbey beside the little river Burn, with the rather hemmed-in remains of the choir and the crossing. The nave has entirely vanished and the remains of the monastic quarters, although visible, are in the private gardens of the adjoining Abbey Farm.

North Creake
Pleasant village in the quiet valley of the Burn, with woodlands on the eastern slopes of the hillside above the church. This is a large 15th century building with tall tower and splendid hammer-beam roof to the nave... a highly imaginative piece of work with angels everywhere (compare with the Victorian reproduction in the chancel). See also the brass to Sir William Calthorpe (1500), with Sir William holding a model of the church.

Egmere Church
Here are the picturesque ruins of a 14th century church on a small grassy mound, with a pond and farm nearby.

Great Walsingham
Now the smaller and less well known of the two Walsinghams, it has a beautiful 14th century church on its northern edge. Its chancel has disappeared and the altar now stands in the nave below the blocked in chancel arch. There are beautifully traceried windows, lovely old benches and bench ends, and an old brick and tiled floor... all contributing to the marvellous flavour of the past lingering here.

Beyond the church is a little green with oak trees and a cross, and beyond this, a ford... all very attractive.

Little Walsingham
In 1061 a certain Lady Richeld saw a vision commanding her to build a replica of the House of Nazareth. A shrine was built and eventually incorporated into the Augustinian abbey, which had become its guardian. By the 15th century Walsingham, as a place of pilgrimage, had not only an English, but a European reputation. Pilgrims came in their thousands, most of whom shed their slippers at the last wayside shrine and walked onwards barefoot... hence the Slipper Chapel at Houghton St. Giles*. At the Reformation all was disbanded, but the concept of 'Our Lady of Walsingham' was revived in the 1890's and in 1931–37 a new Shrine was built.

The Abbey, or more accurately, the Priory church remains stand in the garden of an 18th century house incorporating part of the monastic quarters, and its gatehouse still survives. However to many people, Little Walsingham's charms centre upon the small streets, with their 16th century half timbered, brick houses, and the square (The Common Place) with its medieval, brick, pump house, and its delightful little Shirehall Museum.   *This is now a Roman Catholic Shrine.

Little Walsingham Church and Great Snoring (See Page 31)

1. Egmere Church

2. The Shrine, Walsingham

3. The Gateway Walsingham Abbey

4. The Common Place, Little Walsingham

5. The Rectory, Little Walsingham

6. The Rectory, Great Snoring

Map 15

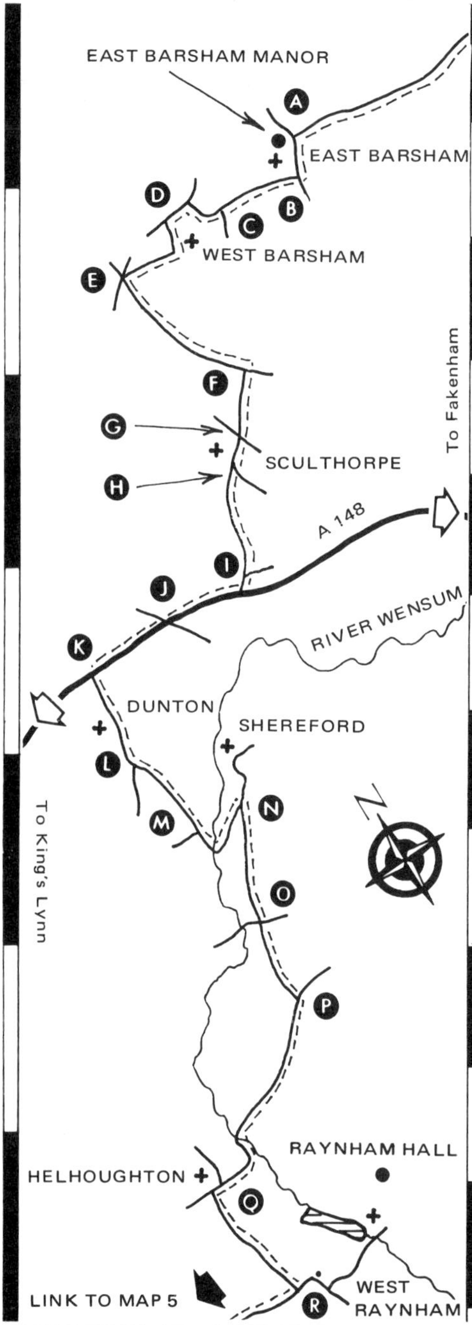

Ref	kms/Miles	Directions	Sign-posted
	1.4	Enter East Barsham	
A	.2	Turn left on to B1105, by bridge over River Stiffkey	No sign
	.1	East Barsham Manor on right (NOT open to the Public)	
B	.1	Turn right by church	West Barsham
C	.4	Straight, not left, at T junction	No sign
	.2	Turn left at T junction	Fakenham
D	.2	Turn left at T junction beyond farm in West Barsham (WATCH FOR THIS WITH CARE...VERY EASY TO MISS THIS TURNING)	No sign
	.2	Turn right at X rds. by church	No sign
E	.3	Turn left at 5 way cross, and... Left again	Fakenham
F	.8	Turn right at T junction	Sculthorpe
G	.3	Over X rds, crossing B1355	Sculthorpe
	.1	Sculthorpe entry signed Church on right	
H	.1	Fork right	'Moor Lane'
I	.6	Bear right, and immediately... Right again, on to A148	Dunton / King's Lynn
J	.4	Over offset X rds., keeping on A148	King's Lynn
K	.6	Turn left at T junction off A148	Dunton
	.1	Straight, not right, at Y junction	No sign
	.2	Dunton church on right	
L	.2	Straight, not right	No sign
M	.4	Straight, not right	Shereford
	.2	Over River Wensum	
N	.3	Turn sharp right at Y junction, by phone box (But go straight ahead if you wish to visit Shereford church)	No sign
O	.6	Over X rds.	Helhoughton
P	.4	Bear right at T junction	Helhoughton
	.3	Pig's Pond Plantation on right	
	.5	Re-cross River Wensum Helhoughton entry signed	
Q	.3	Over X rds. by church	Rudham
	.1	Turn left, opposite the Buck Inn	West Raynham
R	.7	Turn right at T junction in West Raynham	East Rudham
		(LINKING WITH MAIN CIRCLE ROUTE AT MAP 5, POINT O)	
		Total mileage on this map: 10.3	

CROWN COPYRIGHT RESERVED

On Route

Little Walsingham Church (See Page 28)
Was gutted by fire in 1961, but has been lavishly and most effectively restored... what an extraordinary contrast in appeal, with that of Great Walsingham. Luckily the superb Seven Sacrament font survived, along with several interesting brasses. See also the carving by Epstein of The Risen Christ.

Great Snoring (See Page 28)
Pretty village with bright cottage gardens and a church standing in a large churchyard, with flowering cherries bordering the path to the south porch. The unspoilt interior has a screen with interesting early painting, and some quaint early 19th century 'Commandment Boards' with folk art figures. The lovely rectory beyond the churchyard used to be the manor house (1525), and its moulded mellow brickwork is similar in style to East Barsham (see below).

East Barsham
Here in the Stiffkey valley is one of Norfolk's loveliest manor houses... a splendid 16th century building in moulded mellow brick, complete with two-storeyed gatehouse, and a truly wonderful assortment of turrets and chimneys. (Please do not intrude. This house is definitely NOT OPEN to the Public.) A little further up the hill, beyond the attractively painted White Horse Inn, is East Barsham church, a sadly abbreviated building, with no chancel, and a truncated tower, serving as a porch.

West Barsham
There are Anglo-Saxon origins to this tiny, rebuilt church. Its restoration has been carried out in the simplest of styles and is most pleasing to the eye. The entire surroundings are immaculate and are, we assume, under the kindly eye of the Lord of the Manor.

Sculthorpe
The church here was almost entirely re-built by the Victorians, but if you find it locked, obtain the key from the verger, who lives in one of the cottages to the left of our route, for inside is a particularly fine Norman font, one side of which depicts the Adoration of the Magi. There are also two brasses and an 18th century organ, which came from no less a place than the Assembly Rooms at York.

Dunton
Minute hamlet whose small church has no special features of interest.

Shereford
Has a Norman church, whose squat round tower overlooks quiet meadows beyond the willow bordered Wensum. It has a Norman south doorway, and a circular Norman font, but little else of interest.

Helhoughton
An undistinguished village with a small 14th century church. Its nave was restored and re-built in the late 18th century, and the pulpit would appear to be of the same period.

1. East Barsham Manor

2. From West Barsham Porch

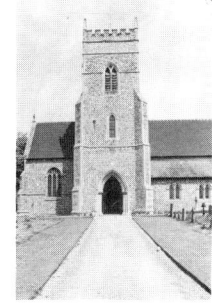

3. Sculthorpe Church

4. Shereford Church

5. Road to Helhoughton

INDEX

Agrarian Revolution 13, 21	Erpingham 4	Old Hunstanton 17
Alby 5	Felbrigg Hall 3	Oulton Street 6
Alby Crafts 5	Flitcham 15	Peddar's Way 1, 13, 17
Appleton 15	Flitcham Abbey 14	Pigs Pond Plantation 30
Atkinson 11	Fountains family 7	Plumstead 27
Babingley Valley 15	Glaven estuary 25	Pocohontas, Princess 17
Baconsthorpe 27	Godwick Hall 11	Raynham Hall 13
Baconsthorpe Castle 27	Great Snoring 31	Reepham 7
Barrow Common 19	Great Walsingham 29	Repton, Humphrey 3
Barry, Charles 9	Great Witchingham 9	Richeld, Lady 29
Bawdeswell 9	Gresham, John 27	Ripley, Thomas 27
Beeston Regis 3	Gresham School 27	Rolfe, John 17
Beeston Regis Priory 3	Gun Hill 21	'Roman Camp', The 3
Binham 23	Hackford church 7	Roubiliac 11
Binham Priory 23	Haggard's Lodge 28	Roughton 5
Birdland Aviaries 5	Hanworth 5	Salle 7
Blakeney 23	Hanworth Hall 5	Salthouse 25
Blakeney Point 23	Harpley 13	Sandringham 15
Blickling 5, 7	Hastings, Sir Hugh 9	Scolt Head Island 19, 21
Blickling Hall 7	Heacham 17	Sculthorpe 31
Bloggs, Henry 3	Helhoughton 31	Shereford 31
Boleyn Family 7	Hempstead Woods 26	Sheringham 3
Brancaster 19	Heydon, Sir Henry 25, 27	Slipper Chapel 29
Brancaster Staithe 19	Heydon, Sir William 27	Snettisham 17
Branodunum 19	Hillington 15	South Raynham 11
Briggs family 7	Hobart, Sir Henry 7	Stanfield 11
Brisley 11	Holme-next-the-Sea 13, 17	Stiffkey valley 31
Bure, River 5	Holkham 21	Stone, Nicholas 11, 21
Burgh-le-Marsh 13	Holkham Hall 21	Suffolk, Earl of 7
Burn, River 29	Holt 27	Surrey, Earl of 11
Burnham Deepdale 19	Howard, Henry 15	Swanton Morley 9
Burnham Market 21	Houghton Hall 13	Thornham 19
Burnham Overy 21	Houghton St. Giles 29	Thornham Creek 19
Burnham Thorpe 21	Hunstanton 17	Thornham Harbour 17, 19
Butterfield 27	Hunstanton Hall 17	Thwaite 5
Buttlands, The 21	Ingoldisthorpe 15	Titchwell 19
Bylaugh 9	Ingworth 5	Tittleshall 11
Calthorpe 5	Kelling Heath 25	Townsend, Sir Charles 13
Calthorpe, Sir William 29	Kelling Park Aviaries 25	Townsend, Sir Roger 13
Campbell, Colin 13, 27	Kent, William 21	Townsend, 'Turnip' 13
Castle Acre 11, 13	Ketton-Cremer, K. W. 3	Trinity Hospital 15
Castle Rising 15	La Neve, Oliver 7	Upcher, Abbot 25
Cawston 7	Langham 23	Upper Sheringham 25
Chaucer's House 9	Langham Glass House 23	Walpole, Horatio 27
Chelmsford 13	Le Strange family 17	Walpole, Sir Robert 13, 17
Cley-next-the-Sea 25	Little Barningham 27	Walsingham Abbey 29
Coke family 11	Little Walsingham 29	Walsingham, Our Lady of ... 29
Coke of Norfolk 21	Little Walsingham church 31	Warham All Saints 23
Coke, Lord Chief Justice .. 11, 21	Mannington Hall 27	Warham St. Mary 23
Creake Abbey 29	Mill Street 9	Wash, The 13
Crossdale Street 2	Morston Quay 23	Wellingham 11
Cromer 3, 5	Nelson, Edmund 21	Wells-next-the-Sea 21
De la Pole, Sir Michael 7	Nelson, Horatio 21	Wensum, River 9, 31
Dersingham 15	New Houghton 13	West Barsham 31
De Warenne, William 11	Nollekens 11	West Newton 15
Duel Stone, The 7	Norfolk, Bishop of 9	West Raynham 13
Dunton 31	Norfolk Coast Path 1, 13, 17	West Runton 3
East Barsham 31	Norfolk Shire Horse Centre ... 3	Weybourne 25
East Raynham church 13	Norfolk Wildlife Park 2	Weybourne Hope Beach 24
Edge, William 13	Northampton, Earl of 15	Whitwell church 7
Egmere church 29	North Creake 29	Wolterton Hall 27
Elsing 9	North Elmham 9	Wyndham Park 5
Epstein 31	North Norfolk Railway 3, 25	